Cordelia Knott

Pioneering Business Woman

Christiane Victoria Salts

The Literature Connection Books

The Literature Connection
PO Box 5278, Buena Park, CA 90622–5278

All possible efforts were made to secure permission and ensure proper credit given for the information in this book. Photo Credits: All photos were taken from the Orange County Archives and Author's Archive unless otherwise stated. Design: Cover and layout was produced by Richard Robert Clarke V.

ISBN 978–0–9842250–0–2

1st printing ..... October 2009
2nd printing .... December 2009

The Literature Connection was established in July of 1988 in Buena Park, CA. Our mission is to promote literacy among young people and adults.

To all the Knott Family members, especially
those who worked at the "Farm" over the years –
they collectively made a dream real for all of us

To the many dedicated current and former
employees of the Chicken Dinner Restaurant

To my loving husband and key supporter
Dennis, my awesome daughters Carrie and Tracy,
my sister Uta and to my wonderful mother Victoria

May the legacy of Cordelia and Walter Knott
live on in our minds, hearts, and at the Farm

Knott's Berry Place in the 1930s

Contents

The Knott family in the Berry Market

Preface
Who was Cordelia Knott?

Cordelia in rural Illinois school – 1899

Have you ever thought of doing something that others told you was far-fetched or would be hard to achieve? Maybe you wanted to learn a new skill, reach a certain score in a sport, or find a way to sell something you made. If you tried hard and reached your goal, you could call yourself "determined." The person this book is about was just that, and much more.

Cordelia Hornaday was born on January 23, 1890, in Bushton, Illinois. Her mother died when she was just 11. In order to cope, she learned to be self-reliant and strong. Cordelia graduated from high school, but never had the chance to go to school for extra training afterwards. She was self-taught and had a knack for working with food to make it presentable and tasty. Today we would call her a master chef, even though she never went to culinary school.

This is the story of her life, and how she built a successful business from scratch. It was to become a world-famous venture. This is also the story of her marriage to Walter Knott and how they worked together with the help of their four children and many others to keep the history of their western ancestors alive.

Train station in Illinois

Chapter One
From Country Town to California

Steam Engine

The clickety-clacking of the train on the track made Cordelia feel sleepy. She stared out of the window, her eyes moving back and forth over the endless grassy plains, searching for something other than just flat land. She pondered, *If only there were some hills or mountains, or at least more houses and trees, then it wouldn't be so boring.* The year was 1904 and this was Cordelia's first train trip across the country.

There was smoke in the air, and the engine came within view as the train pulled around a curve. Cordelia could see the initials of the train on the side — CCC & SL. She knew that one of the C's stood for Chicago and the SL meant St. Louis, where they would be changing trains to head even further west. Every so often, they passed a wooden platform, but the train kept chugging along, just slowing long enough to drop a mail bag and grab the one hanging on an extended pole, ready to be delivered further down the line.

Just as Cordelia wondered if they were ever going to stop, the train brakes suddenly screeched and brought them to a halt in the middle of nowhere. Cordelia and her younger sister Rachel watched as local farmers loaded bushels of corn and potatoes, and sacks of wheat and hay grown and harvested on their plots, to be sold in the bigger towns up the way. Chickens cackled as their wooden crates were jostled onto the boxcar platforms. *Those poor hens don't know what's ahead for them! They'll be sold at the local farmer's markets just like the ones I've seen in our own hometown.* Cordelia cringed as she pictured the town butchers chopping off their heads. Just as quickly as the train had stopped, it suddenly lurched forward and picked up speed.

Rachel had nodded off and was leaning her head on Cordelia's shoulder. Her father John's face was hidden behind his newspaper across from her. She tried to keep from thinking about the events of the past three years — her mother Martha's death at the young age of 44, her father's attempts to cook and cope with her sister's bouts of sobbing at the oddest times. Cordelia had grown up fast. She really was a substitute mother, as her mother was no longer with them. She now had to do the things pioneer women had to do — bake bread, make soap, do the laundry by hand, and do all the things like sewing and making clothes for her sister and herself. She had learned skills like needlework, ironing with a flatiron, and making a pie from her mother Martha. She couldn't have imagined how handy these skills would later become to her as her future life unfolded.

Maybe it's best I keep looking out the window and focus on what might be coming around the next curve, Cordelia thought. She saw corn that grew taller than a man between the endless fields of grain and wheat bound neatly and scattered around the plots of land that had already been threshed. She saw cattle roaming and grazing, basking in the noonday sun. She saw farmhouses next to their trademark red barns with grain elevators set to the side of them.

Finally, the train came to a halt in a town that seemed bigger than her hometown of Bushton, Illinois. Cordelia, her sister and their father caught a whiff of biscuits baking as they stepped off the train for a stretch. Looking across the street, they saw a boarding house with windows ajar. *Oh, those smell just like the buttermilk biscuits Mama used to make.* Cordelia got a lump in her throat as she recalled helping her Mom roll out and cut out the biscuits, and how they melted in her mouth when she ate them piping hot with butter and jam.

The wooden sidewalk creaked and groaned with the weight of the train folks walking up and down, as they stared into the shop windows admiring the fancy goods. Cordelia nearly jumped out of her shoes when she almost bumped into an Indian who was coming out of a tobacco shop. She had never seen a live Indian before. *He looks a lot like the pictures I've seen, but where is his headdress?* With her heart still racing, she grabbed Rachel by the hand and they ran like the wind to get back on the train.

So the train continued on for the four-day journey toward the west coast. Cordelia stared out the window, trying to distract herself by counting the rivers they crossed or by counting how many cows and cattle she saw that day. Every so often, the train would stop to take on water or wood or coal, new cargo would be loaded and some livestock or grains and vegetables would be unloaded. The stretches of land seemed endless between the few times Cordelia and the other passengers were allowed to get off the train. Before very long, the train whistle blew, a bell would clang and the conductor called out, "All aboard!" The friendly uniformed black porter helped Cordelia and Rachel back onto the train steps each time. Again, the train would lurch and move forward, soon whishing past more farms and more towns.

Cordelia's mind drifted and her thoughts landed on the future. *What will high school be like? Will the weather be forever sunny in Southern California like I've heard? Will Pomona be a big city or more rural, like my hometown? Will the roads be paved in gold? Maybe I'll get to do some city things, like I've heard about — go see a picture show, and buy store-bought clothing at the fancy stores… Oh my goodness, that would be an adventure!* Her excitement grew when thinking about the possibilities ahead, but for now, it was enough to imagine that perhaps the next years would hold some hope, because the last few surely weren't easy on her. She had done her best to keep her chin up, for her sister's sake.

Cordelia felt she needed to be strong as the older one, even at her tender age of 14. She acted older than her age because of all she had already been through. It was this sense of self sufficiency that would help to get her through other tough times in her life, and make her a successful leader and businesswoman one day.

Chapter Two
Pomona Possibilities

Early 1900s classroom

Who was that lean and lanky-looking boy who had just stared at her from two aisles over in her 9th grade typing class? She dared not stare back right away, but she snuck a peek, waited a few more minutes, and then took another quick glance. He flashed a shy grin, and she could see his translucent blue eyes peering out from behind his thin horn-rimmed glasses. She could feel a blush rising. *Oh, do you suppose, did he really notice me?* Cordelia's thoughts raced. *Wait — wasn't he the very boy who zoomed past me on his bike on the playground and called me Mary? He must have mistaken me for someone else. I wondered why he rode off so quickly. I'll have to tell Rachel about this. I'll have to ask my other friends what they've heard about him.*

Cordelia cut a fine figure in her dress with her tiny waist shown off by a wide sash. These were the early days of the twentieth century, when girls wore long dresses and admired boys their age from a distance. Her green eyes were lively in contrast to her light brown hair. She was considered to be pretty and had more than once caught admiring looks from young men. But she noticed that this young man seemed different. He didn't goof off like the others in the class. He was intent on his assignments and seemed to be serious-minded. As she would later find out, Walter Knott was a very determined person and was set on working hard to reach his goals. He reminded Cordelia of her father, John, and she loved her father very much.

One of Cordelia's friends reported that she knew Walter from church, where she often saw him at Wednesday evening prayer meetings as well as in Sunday services, and he even had been a church janitor in 5th and 6th grades. Another of her friends shared that Walter sometimes came to the front door to collect money because he delivered their newspaper, the *Pomona Progress*. Walter, it seemed, was already an entrepreneur.

Cordelia thought to herself, *I wonder what he does for fun? Does he work all the time? Why does he work so hard? I don't see him playing on the streets like the other boys very often do, or riding his bicycle back and forth in a nonsensical manner. He only rides his bike to get to school.*

Then one day, Cordelia happened to be walking home on a different path and she caught a view of Walter in a vegetable garden behind a hedge. He was raking the dirt between some rows of carrots and onions with a hoe. Even though he was bent over, his tall slim frame made him seem older than his 16 years. Cordelia's heart stopped, and she felt a rush of butterflies in her stomach. *What if he sees me? I hope he doesn't catch me staring at him!* But just then, Walter stopped to lean on his hoe and suddenly noticed Cordelia. His face broke out in a shy smile. Cordelia smiled back but felt embarrassed and hurried on her way. He seemed more relaxed and comfortable here in the outdoors than in school, doing paperwork.

The next day, Cordelia told her friends about the after-school incident. One of them said, "Didn't you know? His father died when he was only six years old! Ever since then, he's worked to earn money to help the family." Now it made sense to her why she never saw him playing. Cordelia was impressed with his resourcefulness.

So they definitely had something in common, both having lost a parent. Although he was shy and often didn't know what to say, Walter Knott was always friendly to Cordelia Hornaday after their first chance encounters, and she took a liking to him. Their friendship grew over the next two years. So it was sad news when Cordelia found out that Walter was not going to stay in high school after tenth grade. She was shocked and surprised, and so was Walter's mother.

Walter would spend the next two years as a field worker in the Imperial and Coachella Valleys, working very hard to prove to himself and others that he could make his own way by farming. Walter's determination was real, but he could never stop thinking about the pretty and lively Cordelia, back in

Bringing in the harvest

Pomona. In fact, they wrote letters back and forth during those two long years from 1907 to 1909, and kept each other up-to-date on what was happening. Walter told of how his crops of peas and other vegetables were finally growing, even after a bad problem with frost, and how he paid the Indian workers with silver coins because they didn't trust paper money.

Cordelia wrote back about all the special events going on in high school, and how she was sad that he was not able to take part in the many fun activities. But those two long years of lonely work for Walter paid off in the end when he realized he had saved almost $500 in hard-earned cash. Now that he had proven himself, he could come back to Pomona with his chin up and his head held high.

Chapter Three
"Cordy"

The shy couple

One summer day, Cordelia was surprised to see Walter when he stopped in at the Pomona telephone office where she worked. *He looks so tan and tall now. Wait until I tell Rachel. He's so handsome and adult-like!*

Butterflies fluttered in her stomach and she was suddenly without words. Walter seemed more confident and self-assured than she remembered him from before, when they were in high school. He acted friendly and cordial to her and her co-workers.

Walter was now working just nine miles north of Pomona at a

lemon grove. During that summer, he rode down on his bike to see Cordelia after work whenever he could. Soon, he started to tease her by saying, "Cordy, when are you going to marry me?" With a blush and a smile, she would shyly reply, "Walter, you know I'm too little!" *He sure likes to tease me, but I just love how I feel inside when he calls me "Cordy,"* she thought.

Soon, Walter took a better-paying job as a cement contractor in Pomona. He was now living closer, but worked long hours, even into the night. So now, Cordelia and Walter saw each other only whenever they could get the same days off work. Cordelia was especially pleased when, on such occasions, Walter showed up at her doorstep to take her on a horse and buggy ride.

Back then, very few people had automobiles as yet, and young couples courted by riding around in horse-drawn wagons. It was a high point of the week to go for a Sunday drive. They would wave at friends who were strolling along the street. Sometimes, Walter parked their rented buggy by the side of the road, helped Cordelia step down, and then they would take a long stroll on the trails in the park. *I feel so safe and secure holding onto Walter's arm. I hope this day lasts forever!*

On a Sunday outing

A few times, Cordelia fixed up a picnic basket, and she and Walter sat on the grassy side of a gently sloped hill to enjoy their feast. Walter was impressed with the delicious lunch she had packed for them. The fried chicken and biscuits tasted ever so good washed down with ice-cold lemonade. *I hope he likes my thumbprint grape jelly cookies, too.* Cordelia was tickled when she noticed Walter smile and smack his lips happily after devouring the cookies. She felt special when he brought her candy and they went to the concerts in the park. It was at these times of leisure that they talked at length, and Walter told Cordelia of his dreams to own his own land and farm it. His excitement made Cordelia joyful. Her hopes for a future together with this young man were soon to come true.

Cordelia and Walter were married on a hot summer day in June of 1911, when they were both 21 years old. They were nervous, but also very happy. They had a new house to call their own, which Walter had built on West Fourth Street in Pomona. They went to the church Walter's father had helped to start. Walter was now

Married at last!

a foreman with the cement company and was paid well. Cordy easily took on the role of wife, cooking fine meals for her husband to enjoy when he came home. Both of them were very happy and felt like they had the whole world in their hands.

Just three days after she turned 23 years old, Cordelia gave birth to Virginia Maurine Knott on January 26, 1913. Walter was proud

Cordelia with baby Virginia

as punch of his wife and their new daughter, who was named after his mother. Cordelia happily settled into the role and tasks of being a mother without missing a beat. She imagined how nice it would be if they had more children and they could attend the same school she and Walter went to, and maybe even go to college in Pomona as well. Her dreams were finally coming to life. Little did she know what the next few years would bring, and that her new little family would soon be uprooted.

Chapter Four
Seeking Self-Reliance

Dressed up for Sunday

Cordelia was content in her life as wife and mother, but she noticed that Walter was not always happy in his job. He did not like the great amount of paperwork and the long office hours. He yearned to be outdoors in the fields, smelling the fresh air and observing the various farmers in the area. He kept talking about his dream of owning his own farm and working on the land. Walter didn't mind getting his hands dirty or working up a sweat, like some people did. He liked to be out with his overalls on and his boots, rather than being dressed up in some stiff suit. He regretted that he wasn't able to get the farm his mother had to sell off after his father had died, but they just didn't have the money and the bank wouldn't loan it to them either. After all, Walter was just a young man. With no adult man on the farm, how could they possibly make it — the bankers wondered. So the bank would not give them the loan.

Walter spoke often of when he worked in the Coachella Valley, which was desert at one time, but now had rich farmland on it because of the hard work that people had done there. And then one day, he said, "Cordy, let's go to the Mojave Desert and stake out a homestead claim of land for ourselves. We could own 160 acres of land if we live on it for three years and make improvements!" Cordelia couldn't believe what she was hearing. "You don't really mean that, do you?" she asked. But he was dead serious. *What is he thinking? We have our house right here where everything is so easy to get to in the city and he has a good-paying job! In the winter, in the windy, hot desert, it would be a really hard life, and in the summer, even hotter! Besides, there are snakes and coyotes and scorpions and, Lord knows what else!*

It took one year before Cordelia realized there was no use in her trying to hold Walter back from his dream of being a farmer on his own land.

So in 1914, with little one-year-old Virginia on her lap, Cordelia found herself riding on a wagon over the bumpy desert road for five seemingly endless miles, going west from the Santa Fe train station in Newberry, California, to the desert home they would call their own for the next three years. *I don't see any other houses along the way. There's nothing here but dry brush and rocks! Oh, dear, what has Walter got us into now?*

During the long ride, both Walter and Cordelia were quiet and wondering what the desert life held in store for them. They knew they could work harder than anybody else. He knew how to be a farmer and she knew how to be a housewife and do all the things that need to be done. *What is it really going to be like, though? What is God going to hand us? It seems like it's going to be hard, really hard. What kind of weather will we have to put up with, what kind of pests?*

Finally, they arrived at their Mojave homestead, which was 25 miles east of Barstow. Cordy's heart sank as she looked around while Walter unloaded the wagon and brought the mattress and blankets inside. That was all the furniture they had brought with them. *This house has only two rooms! There's no running water and no indoor bathroom!*

Indeed, the adobe house was very humble and Cordelia swallowed her pride as she set out to make it into a home. She worked inside the house, trying to keep it clean from the constant sand that swirled around. The sand blew in through the crack under the door. There was no way to keep the house clean like she could back in Pomona, try as she might. Outside, Walter braved the hot desert sun on 100-degree days, weeks at a time. Every day he had to haul water from the windmill well to the house and then brought water from the deeper well to the grapevines he had planted. But just as the vines were about to produce grapes, a windstorm pulled them out of the ground. In the desert, he realized, the wind is relentless.

This was the first of many trials and setbacks on this desert "farm." The deep well filled up with sand over and over again. The Knott family only had milk from their one cow and some eggs from their few chickens once in a while. Walter finally realized that trying to farm in the desert is not possible without a heavy-duty well, which they could not afford, and so he began to do odd jobs like making adobe bricks for other homesteaders.

In 1915, Walter heard workers were needed at the abandoned Calico Ghost Town about 35 miles away, going north from Barstow in the direction of Nevada. Walter took on work as a carpenter, helping to rebuild the mill where they used to mine silver 35 years earlier, in the 1880s and 1890s. This job took him away from home and so Cordelia, expecting their second child, was left home alone for days at a time. The closest neighbors were one half mile away, hardly close enough to hear a shout for help if something went wrong. Cordy had to trudge to the well for water several times a day, and the pail felt as heavy as if she were carrying rocks on the way back to the house. She wondered when her back would stop hurting. *I wonder if all this lifting and carrying is going to hurt my baby or bring on the labor too soon. I want my baby and my family to be healthy. I'm tired of lugging water. I wish we had indoor plumbing like we did in Pomona.* Cordelia yearned for city life once again.

Chapter Five
A Growing Family

Cordelia with Russel and Virginia

Walter knew that Cordelia needed him to help, so he quit his job just in time to travel with his family back to Pomona for the birth of their second baby. On January 10, 1916, Cordelia gave birth to a son and they named him Russell. Little three-year-old Virginia was tickled pink to have a baby brother to play with!

Back at home in the desert, both parents settled into their routine of trying to make a go of it in a hostile desert environment. The winds and sandstorms were relentless, the dust was everywhere. Cordelia did everything she could to keep the dirt out of the house, but sometimes the food even tasted like sand was mixed in with it. *Oh, dear! I'm running out of ideas of how to cover up the dusty taste of everything!*

Walter found out about a job that paid better than the last one, doing road construction work to build a road from Newberry to Needles. There were railroad stops in both towns, and this is where farmers brought their products to be sold and shipped. The roads were needed for use by the farmers to drive their wagons to local stations and markets.

Again, because they needed the money, Walter ended up working away from home and leaving Cordelia alone with the children. But after one year of this job, they had saved over $300, which was a good deal of money in those days.

Soon after little Russell had turned one, second daughter Rachel Elizabeth was born on January 25, 1917. Now four-year-old Virginia had two little playmates and companions!

Being the oldest, Virginia was often relied upon to help watch her little sister and brother while their mother did the outside chores or was busy with an occasional visitor. Their neighbor Margaret walked the half mile in the desert heat to visit with them and to sew. The ladies of that day often made their own clothing, as there was no money for buying store-bought clothing. They had to make do with what they had, to repair and patch it up and make it last. Hand-me-downs were common then, so that little baby Rachel got to use the clothes that no longer fit Virginia. Cordelia had a sewing machine, and Virginia watched closely as her mom and the visitors made themselves pretty Sunday dresses and, on occasion, even some new clothes for the children to wear.

Sewing was a skill Cordelia had brought with her to the desert.

However, there were things she had to learn by figuring them out on her own in order to survive. She needed milk for her children, and so she learned how to milk a cow on her own. She tried to feed her family fresh food, but many times had no greens of any kind to go with the meager meals. Trying to grow vegetables in the desert just didn't work out. The roots of the trees, grapes and vegetables just couldn't reach down far enough to keep from being torn out of place by the winds. As Cordelia later said to her good friend Margaret, "The only good thing we raised in the desert was a fine bunch of children!"

It was only on special occasions, for birthdays or Sunday dinners when guests came, that Cordelia would bake an apple pie for dessert. Very rarely, Walter brought home some Macintosh baking apples that he was lucky enough to get at a good price from a farmer's stand on the way back from his construction work. Other times, Cordelia had to use dried apples that had been sent by her sister Rachel in a birthday package, or that she brought back from Pomona herself. These chewy dried apples tasted very sweet, and little Russell had gotten his hand slapped more than once when he managed to reach up to the kitchen counter and grab some slices of apple that were being soaked in water to prepare for the making of a dried apple pie. After Cordelia had made the pie crust, she let Virginia help roll out the extra leftover dough and sprinkle it with cinnamon spice before baking. The children delighted in having their own baked spice crust for dessert, while Cordelia and Walter and their guests enjoyed the special treat of apple pie after dinner.

The growing Knott family had to stay close and help together in order to survive against the desert elements. It was this closeness that would carry them through many times in the future as they survived other challenges too unexpected to predict.

Chapter Six
A Change of Scenery

Farm in Shandon, CA

Three years had passed, and now Walter and Cordelia were landowners of 160 acres of land free and clear in the desert. They had worked very hard at this desert farming and had proven to themselves that they could do something many others had failed to do. One only had to look around the area to see the other settler's shacks and adobes that had been abandoned because they could not survive and stay for the three years. They had lost their claims. But Walter and Cordelia, because of their working together and their perseverance, were able to survive by sheer will and hard work. They had a right to be proud of themselves for earning their claim to this land and therefore they held onto it for many years to come. As Walter later reflected, "The hardships we endured made us tough. After what we went through there, nothing could really faze us."

So they put their things on the wagon, tied the buggy behind, and set out for the new job Walter had arranged on a cattle ranch in San Luis Obispo County, about half way up the California coast between Los Angeles and San Francisco. Virginia was excited to ride in the wagon, but little Russell hung on tightly to the side as they were bounced up and down over the unpaved roads. Cordelia held baby Rachel, whom they had nicknamed Toni, and remembered how three years earlier she had her first child on her lap as they traveled over the same rocky roads to their desert home. Her feelings were mixed. *I'll never forget how lonely I felt when Walter left for that Calico mine job and I had to learn by myself how to milk a cow. I hope I never have to milk a cow again! And I won't miss all that sand, that's for sure. But we've worked so hard out here in the desert and made such close friends — I wonder if we'll ever get to see them again.* Cordelia got a lump in her throat and felt tears welling up in her eyes. But then she thought about the little town Walter had described to her, and her hopes soared. She asked him over and over again about Shandon, where they were headed.

The horses plodded slowly along the highway. They were not used to walking on anything but sand and dirt. They were old and worn out, and so it took three weeks for the Knott family to make the trip to their destination. As they worked their way slowly through Pomona and westward, cars whooshed past them on the road and honked their horns in aggravation because they had to slow down behind the wagon. The automobile age had started and wagons were no longer a common sight. Each night, Walter and

Cordelia set up camp by the roadside and they all slept on the ground on bedrolls next to their wagon. They had to buy milk for the children from the farmhouses they passed.

On a Sunday, as they got to the busy modern city of Pasadena, Walter and Cordelia noticed people coming out of a church service pointing and whistling at them. Walter tried to ignore them. He felt embarrassed about being seen in faded overalls on an old dilapidated wagon that was going ever-so-slowly down the busy fashionable boulevard. All of a sudden, a well-dressed man caught up with their wagon in his limousine and got out. He told Walter that a spring which helped support the wheel of the buggy was dragging on the ground behind their wagon and might soon fall off. Walter fixed the problem and thanked the friendly man. After they chatted, both men gave each other a warm farewell. Walter Knott later said that he learned never to judge a person by first glance or by their outward appearance again.

The Knott family with friends in Shandon, CA

Chapter Seven
Creative Resourcefulness

Russell, Virginia, and Toni in Shandon, CA

When the Knott family finally reached the hilly area between the California coast and the great San Joaquin Valley, they and the horses were completely worn out. They moved into a modest house in Shandon that cost just $8 a month for rent. It was 1917 and the Knott's family would call this their home for the next three years.

Walter farmed seven and a half acres of land as a sharecropper. First, he cleared the fields of millions of weeds and bull nettles by hand. This was very labor-intensive work. Then he dug a big ditch to carry water from the small springs to every corner of the plot he was granted. Next, he planted a variety of seeds and waited for them to produce crops. The harvest was to provide food for the ranch owner and his own family. If there was any extra left over, Walter could sell it and save the money he had earned.

While waiting for six months for the seeds to grow, Walter did odd jobs for the rancher, like fixing broken machines, repairing tanks and doing cement work. Sometimes, the Knott's were given odd types of meat in return for Walter's hard work. One day, young Virginia and Russell squirmed as they saw twenty hog's heads in the kitchen sink. Cordelia cut off the loose skin on their necks and cheeks and sprinkled salt all over for flavor and to preserve them. She cooked the pork along with beans and black-eyed peas, which were one of the main things they could afford to eat. She was a master at using what Walter was able to provide to make meals that were tasty and filling.

Walter with his corn crop

Once the crops grew, the Knott family had an over-abundance of vegetables to choose from: huge cabbages, tall corn, bell peppers, tomatoes, and a variety of beans. Life was getting better. Cordelia now had water readily available inside the house. What a pleasure that was! She no longer had to go outside to a well, and didn't have to worry about fighting with the sand and dust storms of the desert. She now had some free time, and used it to experiment with making fancy homemade candy such as fudge. Soon she was selling her candy creations at the little general store in Shandon. Being in the business allowed her to get more sugar and the earnings she made from her sales were wisely saved. Later, at Christmas, this money helped Walter and Cordelia to buy a used 1917 Model T Ford. Finally, they had a car!

Walter and Cordelia decided to take a trip to Southern California to visit their friends and family. The time there brought up longings for city life in Cordelia. *I wish Virginia could be going to one of these schools that have more teachers and programs. And Russell will be school age next year, too.*

Soon after their trip, Walter got two offers for jobs in Southern California. One was from the cement contractor he had worked for in Pomona and the other was from his cousin Jim Preston, who wanted a farm partner to work alongside him in Buena Park. Cordelia was so excited when Walter wrote a letter to his former boss in Pomona to accept that job, but Walter had a sudden change of heart and decided not to send that letter after all. Cordelia's hopes fell flat. *What will Buena Park be like? It's country area, just like up here in Shandon, from what I hear! Why can't we just go back to what we know, to Pomona, where my relatives and friends are?*

But before she knew it, they had packed up their belongings so that Walter could follow his strong feeling that Buena Park was where they really belonged and were destined to go.

Chapter Eight
The Family is Complete

Marion makes the family complete!

It was now 1920. The Knott family had spent three years in Shandon, California, working on the ranch, but now Walter's burning desire to be a landowner seemed within reach. Just as Cordelia had thought, Orange County was farmland not unlike where they came from, but flatter. There were rows upon rows of orange groves, beet fields and walnut orchards on both sides of the dirt road as they drove south from Los Angeles toward their destination.

Walter and Cousin Jim rented twenty acres for $1,000 a year on a five-year lease and got to work raising berries. They were set on having the biggest berry farm in California.

In the berry fields

Cordelia and Walter found a little house on Crescent Street just south of where Knott's Berry Farm now sits. It was nice and close to Centralia School for the children and it was cheap — just $8 a month to rent. But it had no indoor plumbing — which meant once again, like in the desert, Cordelia had to go get her water from outside the house.

Walter had set up an irrigation system that brought water up and down the rows of plants he and Jim had carefully planted. They waited patiently, as it would take a year for the berries to produce fruit. But the weather that first year was harsh and cold and the crops failed. The next year, the price offered for berries was lowered.

On April 22, 1922, little Marion was born. Now their family was complete! However, Cordelia and Walter had real trouble raising enough food to keep their family of six fed. One day, Cordelia had to butcher their pet goat Betsy, to serve it for dinner. When the family sat down to eat, Russell sadly said, "Poor Betsy." Cordelia noticed that the children had tears in their eyes. *Oh, dear, they'll never be able to swallow with lumps in their throats,* Cordelia thought. And so she removed the meat platter with their beloved pet from the table, never to be seen again.

To help pick up business, Walter built a berry market on Grand Ave., which would later be called Beach Boulevard. He wrapped the berries in clean wrapping paper, instead of newspapers like the other sellers. On weekends, many well-to-do folks on their drive to their summer homes in the beach cities stopped by to buy blackberries, dewberries and youngberries. Local people as well as commuters on their drive to work shopped at the Berry Market during the week. Son Russell could often be seen behind the counter weighing and bagging up the berries for the steady stream of buyers. Even truckers began to use the Berry Market as a rest stop. Walter did lots of advertising and put all his attention into making the crops grow and succeed.

Cordelia was in charge of the house and the children. But one time she got very ill, and Walter had to make sure they all had their lunches before going to school. Lo and behold, there was no clean wrapping paper in the house. So that day, they had to take their lunches to school wrapped in newspaper, held together by a nail! You see, Walter's mind was always focused on his fields of berries.

Walter and Cordelia took the children camping once a year to Santa Ana Canyon and stayed on the river with some friends for one or two nights. That was the extent of their vacations at that time. Walter felt he couldn't wait to get back to the farm and build it bigger and better, and he had no desire to travel.

Knott's Berry Stand on Grand Ave.

By 1927, the five-year lease on the land had run out and so had the two-year extension. Land prices were now sky-high because of a local oil boom. Walter wanted to buy ten acres, but his partner Jim thought the land prices were too high and wasn't willing to take the gamble. He was concerned about the economy, and knew he could buy cheaper land somewhere else. Jim tried to convince

Walter to cancel a pre-made agreement with the landowner, but Walter stuck to his principles and signed a contract to purchase those ten acres at a price more than twice as much as what they had paid for renting the land before. So when Jim left, the Knotts were once again on their own, but were determined as ever to make a go of it.

Walter had a house built for his family on the farm in that year. Cordelia was grateful, thinking to herself; *At least we now have running water and indoor plumbing! We have waited a long time for this. It's too bad we don't have central heating yet. I guess we'll just have to make do and adjust somehow.*

Chapter Nine
The Tea Room is Born

Walter with a flat of dewberries.

By now, the Berry Market had grown to 80 feet, where they sold fresh berries and even had a nursery section to sell berry plants. Again, the Knott family faced more hard times as the stock market crashed in 1929 and the Great Depression started the following year. To Walter and Cordelia, that meant the cost of raising berries was more than they could sell them for, and it also meant less customers came to buy. But the Knott family was not about to give up! Cordelia once again got creative and thought to herself, *I can take the leftover fruit that doesn't get sold quickly and make jam and jelly and even pies, and then sell them.* Walter decided to grow asparagus and artichokes as well as other in-season vegetables to sell. He also grew rhubarb as a filler crop. The children even helped out. They stood on street corners and sold three-pound bundles of rhubarb stalks for a dime each. Trying to gain business, they yelled out "Rhubarb for sale — dime a bunch!"

Soon, one end of the Berry Market became a Tea Room, where customers enjoyed Cordelia's homey kindness as she served them homemade rolls, jam and pies. The Tea Room had five tables and could serve up to twenty customers at one time. The Knott girls were a hit as waitresses. Fourteen-year-old Virginia wrote down people's orders and ten-year-old Toni helped serve the meals, while little Marion drew smiles as she brought out the rolls. When more and more people came to eat there, Cordelia decided to add sandwiches to the menu. The little Tea Room was bursting at the seams as customers lined up at mealtimes. Cordelia now needed to hire local farm women to help in the kitchen, but she resolved not to expand it into a restaurant. She thought to herself, *I'm busy enough as it is. I'm not going to keep adding more to the menu!*

Though she was extremely busy, Cordelia always had time to notice when young or old people needed assistance. Her kindness reached further than customers. She took in two homeless children, and now they had a family of six growing children to feed!

Cordelia and Walter proudly sent their brood of children off to school each morning. Together, the children walked the mile or so to Centralia School, which at that time was located on Holder Road. It was a humble two-story building standing alone in an open field. The two classrooms downstairs housed first through sixth grades, and the seventh and eighth grades met in the classroom near the stage upstairs.

On cold mornings, the children huddled close to the wood-burning stove as they entered their classroom. The school had no running water, and there was an outhouse on the playground. It was a typical historical schoolhouse, with a big bell outside on the roof that had a long rope dangling down to the first floor. When a lightweight child would try to ring it, the pull of the bell often lifted them right off the floor. This adventure made the job of bell-ringing the most popular chore, the classroom job every child wanted to have a chance to do!

Around 1930, a man from the United States Department of Agriculture named George Darrow came to visit Walter. He had heard that Mr. Knott was an expert berry grower. Mr. Darrow had also heard of an enormous berry that was a cross between a loganberry, a blackberry and a red raspberry, which a man named Rudolph Boysen had tried to develop. Walter and Mr. Darrow found Mr. Boysen in Anaheim and learned that he had tried to grow the experimental berry long ago, but had given up. Both George Darrow and Rudolph Boysen agreed that if anyone could bring the dying vines back to health, Walter was the one! Walter carefully nursed the six scraggly vines over a period of two years and when successful, he named them boysenberries in honor of Rudolph Boysen. They soon became popular and were in demand because of their big size, as big as a thumb.

Walter & Russell with their boysenberries

Ads for boysenberries were everywhere! Magazines, newspapers, farm and nursery journals — all showed pictures of the giant boysenberry, and told about its great flavor. Some of the magazines featured Cordelia's own recipes showing how to use the boysenberries in pies and with other dishes. One such ad quoted

Cordelia as saying: "I can at last recommend my own recipes to you with the assurance that you will be delighted with the results if you follow the simple directions using your own Knott's Berry Farm boysenberries." This is the berry that Walter made famous, and it was a real blessing for them and many other farmers during those lean Depression years.

Walter had figured out how to quick-freeze fruits and vegetables and he wrote about his methods and findings. He was always willing to share what he had learned as a result of his trial and error plant experiments. By the mid-1930s, Walter and his field crew of 25 young Buena Park workers bundled the plants together to send out in the mail to people all over the USA and even around the world. Knott's Berry Farm was becoming well-known as being one of this nation's biggest berry-plant businesses!

Chapter Ten
What a Bargain!

We are here to serve

    Walter walked along the lines of customers standing outside the Berry Farm Tea Room, waiting their turn. One customer said to him, "What is that smell? It smells so delicious!" Walter answered, "Oh, that's my wife Cordelia frying chicken for our dinner." The customer asked, "Is that on the menu in the Tea Room?" Walter had to explain that Cordelia was only willing to cook for the Tea Room for the time being, in order to make ends meet. The customers expressed their disappointment.

    "What am I going to do? The hungry customers keep lining

up, and lots of them are asking when we're going to start serving dinners!" Cordelia was restless as this thought kept pestering her. So one day she took a big step and asked Walter to bring her some nice fat three and a half pound chickens to fry up. Pulling out

Happy Diners

their wedding china and linen napkins, Cordelia had the girls set up the dining table to serve eight people that very first time in 1934. For 65 cents each, the diners were served cherry rhubarb in sauce dishes, green salad with French dressing, and then fried chicken, mashed potatoes with gravy, boiled cabbage with bits of ham, and hot biscuits served with jam.

Berry pie slices were served for dessert, along with vanilla ice cream or sherbet. By the end of the summer of that year, Cordelia and her helpers were cooking and serving an average of 85 chicken dinners a day. Cordelia was often given compliments on her cooking by the customers. She would answer, "It's just homemade, just like you'd make it yourself." She was always humble and modest when her talents were brought to light.

Two years later, more rooms were added to the Tea Room so that 70 diners could be served at once. They were given hand-lettered menus designed by Toni as they were shown to their tables. Cordelia and her children worked hard trying to keep up

Abuzz with activity

with the demand of the long lines of people waiting to eat. Russell ran outside to catch the chickens which Walter killed and cleaned.

Cordelia then fried the chickens, Virginia and Toni served them, and little Marion took the dishes away.

It was expected and understood that the Knott children would pitch in and help out, but Cordelia was practical enough to know what would keep them willing to work. She thought, *Maybe we'll pay them each something, so they feel like real workers.* So she and Walter started paying each child a "salary" out of which they had to budget money to buy their clothes and schoolbooks. At that time, 25 cents an hour seemed like a lot of money to the children, and being paid made them feel like grown-ups!

The Great, LUSCIOUS BOYSENBERRY (Enlarged Sligh

MENU....

TEA ROOM

KNOTT'S BERRY PLACE

BUENA PARK . . . (Telephone Anaheim 2608) . . . CALIFOR

Here's a Picture of Our Place – So You Can Remember Us Easily

Tea Room Menu 1934 – 1936

One day, a young mother came and was hired to work as a waitress in Mrs. Knott's Tea Room. Vannie was a very hard worker, just like Cordelia, and was soon well-respected. She noticed how business-like and demanding Mrs. Knott was in the kitchen, and so she tried to do her best every day. She wore her hairnet and stockings to work, and put on her apron as soon as she clocked in. She followed instructions carefully because she wanted to please Mrs. Knott and not frustrate her. She saw how, sometimes, those who forgot to do what they had been told, had to be warned in front of the other waitresses and workers. She saw how their faces turned red with embarrassment.

Vannie also saw another side of Cordelia. Her boss was always giving things to the employees to take home to their children. If there was chicken left over, Cordelia sent it home with the waitresses or other kitchen workers for their families. When workers got sick, sometimes Cordelia would take them to the hospital, and even at times she paid the doctor bills when she knew they couldn't afford to pay themselves. Cordelia went to jail to bail out waitresses, took clothes to people whose houses had burned, took groceries to the poor, but she always told Vannie not to let others know about it. Cordelia gave without wanting to get anything in return. She didn't want honors or awards either.

Besides being humble, it seemed to Vannie that Mrs. Knott was also very careful about saving money. Cordelia and Walter lived simply, and didn't even have central heating in their house. Both of them got up at about 4 a.m. to work in the kitchen. Cordelia would cut up and fry chicken or use a rolling pin to roll out pie dough. Walter would make and stir the milk gravy for the chicken and dumplings. By working together, they already had a half day's work done by 8 a.m. when the paid workers came on duty. Soon, the kitchen was crowded and steamy with the hustle and bustle of preparing the hearty chicken dinners and side dishes that were served up every day except for Monday and Tuesday, when the Tea Room was closed.

Chapter Eleven
Patience Is a Blessing

Another expansion

Being ever busier with his fields of berries and rhubarb, Walter left the concerns of the Tea Room to Cordelia and their children. But when he noticed the lines of people that waited all the way up Grand Ave. as far as the eye could see, Walter knew that another expansion of the Tea Room would be necessary. So in 1937 his field crew built the biggest expansion yet and the Tea Room opened for year-round service on May 1. They now had a separate kitchen, dining rooms, and a parking lot. They could seat 325 people, and on a typical day they served more than 500 chicken dinners. But on Thanksgiving Day that year, the line of people extended far north all the way to what is now Orangethorpe Avenue, for more than three blocks long. That day, the Tea Room served 1,774 dinners, 355 pies and 8,890 biscuits! Walter and Cordelia marveled at how the people just kept coming, but they didn't have time to think about it too much because they were so busy serving their new and returning customers.

Cordelia was strong-willed and spent many hours in the kitchen. She expected her employees to work just as hard as she did. By now she was depending on 35 neighbor ladies to be her kitchen helpers. She was often heard to say, "If a job is worth doing, it is worth doing right!" If a waitress had a spot on her apron, right away she was told to get a clean one. "You wouldn't serve your guests at home in a dirty apron, would you?" Cordelia scolded them. "Well, these are our guests and they're to be treated just as you'd treat people coming to your home." If they were chewing gum, she might call out their name loudly in front of the other workers and embarrass them. If they weren't wearing a hairnet, it cost them 25 cents.

Although she was strict with them, Cordelia was kind and had a soft spot in her heart for her employees. Many of Cordelia's kitchen workers felt loved by her and felt privileged to belong to her "Breakfast Club" that met one Monday morning each month at a restaurant across the street. Other times, Mrs. Knott and some of her workers drove to the beach after the kitchen cleanup was done. They enjoyed having their pictures taken with Cordelia by

Happy pie makers

a photographer that came along. At those times, they formed a strong bond with each other and with "Mama Knott," as they affectionately called her. But when they were at work back at the

Knott kitchen, they pulled the strings off the string beans, cut up the chickens, mashed the potatoes, made coffee, baked the buttermilk biscuits, cooked the rhubarb, fixed the salads, and dished up the pies. They took pride in their work.

Between their varied kitchen duties, the helpers went out into the rose garden and picked flowers for the vases on the dining tables. On the occasions when Cordelia came out to help them, she always warned, "Don't say my name aloud out here, because then people might hear you." *I don't want people to notice me*, she thought to herself.

Tending to the roses was a life-long interest that both Cordelia and Walter enjoyed. Even when older, they took lessons in rose farming and could at times be spotted taking a walk in the garden, holding hands. The rose garden was Cordelia's pride and joy. A place of peace, it offered a nice change from the busyness of the kitchen.

Another place of refuge for Cordelia was the rock garden, which can be found tucked away behind the Berry Market and is still accessible to visitors. The volcanic rocks were brought from Death Valley and Walter had the crew construct a waterfall and plant ferns on either side.

Oldest daughter Virginia, by now in her mid-twenties, set up a small gift business at the north side of the Tea Room. She sold souvenirs, greeting cards, and handmade items. Patsy Marshall, former Knott's Publicity Director, told of how Cordelia would often put money into Virginia's cash box when Virginia took a break and hadn't sold much of anything yet that day. Her business eventually became Virginia's Gift Shop, which was another favorite stop for visitors of the Farm, as well as for Cordelia!

Chapter Twelve
The Birth of an Idea

The lines kept growing

Walter stood with his left hand on his hip, staring at the long lines of people waiting patiently on Grand Ave. for their turn to be served at the Tea Room, which was by now called the Mrs. Knott's Chicken Dinner Restaurant. With his right hand, Walter pushed his hat back and scratched his head. He was clearly puzzled by the endless streams of customers lined up early in the morning and all day long each day. By the end of 1939, they had served at least 400,000 chicken dinners! This was a long time before Colonel Sanders and fast food was available. This was sort of a miracle in Walter's mind.

It was 1940 now, and with the money they had earned and saved from the berry and restaurant business, Walter and Cordelia were able to pay for all the land they had bought. They no longer had to rent the land they lived on and the berry farm was prospering. They were even able to put some extra money aside because they lived very frugally and didn't do anything extravagant. They still lived in their original house, around which the Chicken Dinner Restaurant had been built. The house still had no central heating or air conditioning.

An idea had been brewing in Walter's head. Here they both were, at the age of 50, having worked hard for the last 30 years. They had managed to survive the Great Depression without getting any help from the government or even depending on banks for a loan. They had come through hard times by rolling up their sleeves, pitching in, and working together as a family, including the children. Now it was time to reflect about the past and look toward the future.

Lately, Walter's mind had drifted back to the stories his grandmother Rosamond Dougherty had told both him and his younger brother Elgin as they sat at her feet by the fireplace. She told them stories about pioneers who pushed themselves and their horses for months at a time, often without water or food, on their way to a better life. During their move out west to the new frontier, these folks ran into all kinds of adventures with Indians and strangers and rattlesnakes. They would gather around campfires at night and sing, weary from the long, hard days. There were all kinds of really interesting things that Walter's grandmother shared and these were stories about the life of a typical person. Hundreds of thousands of people came out west in those days.

Walter had heard about the book called *Little House on the Prairie* that Laurel Ingalls Wilder had written, a book series which tells similar stories. He toyed with an idea — the idea of paying tribute to not only his ancestors, but to all the forefathers who had taken this journey through the Old West to find a better life for themselves and for their children. He thought of recreating an Old West town. If he could build such a thing, then perhaps people would enjoy viewing this kind of a living history display. Knott's Old West Ghost Town was born out of this idea.

Walter had seen an old hotel in Arizona on his travels some time ago, and the vision of that hotel was stuck in his mind. He talked to Cordelia about it. Knowing that once Walter made his mind up, it was no use trying to change it, Cordelia said, "Walter, paying tribute to our ancestors sounds like a fine idea." But also being practical, she said, "Maybe then, the folks that are waiting in such long

The Knott family on the porch of the Gold Trails Hotel

lines for our Chicken Dinner Restaurant will have something to keep them occupied." Walter agreed, and so he arranged for the Gold Trails Hotel to be moved to Knott's Berry Farm from that old Arizona ghost town. The original building had been built back in 1868, the same year his grandparents had traveled overland to settle in California.

The Ghost Town is born!

For the lobby of the hotel, Walter paid a man named Paul Von Klieben to recreate a painted three-dimensional scene, called a cyclorama, showing a covered wagon train on its journey through the desert, with the dramatic mesas of the southwestern deserts on either side of the trail. People were impressed when they viewed this "Covered Wagon Show" and listened to the narrator speak about the hardships and challenges faced by these brave pioneers who traveled to territories that were unfamiliar to them. Many folks shared their delight at having the chance to travel back to that time by watching the show. The former movie actors were hired to create a living history show. They had ladies and gentlemen who depicted the people of the era, wearing detailed costumes of the mid-1800s. There were frontiersmen, Indians, wagon masters, express riders, and people dressed up just like the pioneers who traveled across our great country. Walter felt rewarded when he knew he was keeping a slice of history alive for his grandmother.

Walter and Cordelia were grateful that God had carried them through the hard times in the desert and recently the Depression. In 1941, Walter came up with the idea to make a man-made lake, and next to it he had a chapel built. Artist Von Klieben now took up the challenge to paint a picture called "The Christ" which was the main focus in the chapel. The Little Chapel by the Lake, which seated 50 people, was another favorite spot not just for Cordelia, but also for many people who visited the farm. At age eight, grandson Stephen, the second son of Russell, was given the job of standing at the chapel

The Little Chapel by the Lake

door to be a greeter and open it for park guests. He was paid ten cents a day for this first of many jobs he performed at the park!

Chapter Thirteen
The Ghost Town Expands

Walter & Cordelia Knott with their Train in 1952

The Wild West was a very popular theme in books and movies in the mid-1900s and even later. Roy Rogers and Gene Autry were top box office movie stars for several years. So Walter had hit on a theme that held wide interest for that time. Soon Walter decided to expand his venture, and the Ghost Town added the Blacksmith Shop where they fixed the wagons and the shoes of the horses. The Livery Barn was where horses were boarded, just like a stable. The Wells Fargo Express was a freight company housed in a brick building with iron shutters that would have handled shipments of money and goods. Guests strolling along the wooden boardwalks on either side of the main street in this ghost town might see old-timers like Handsome Brady sitting on the benches, sharing stories of the Old West. Later they would stop at the Ghost Town Boot Hill Cemetery, a favorite spot for children and grown-ups alike. Every child-at-heart wanted the chance to get to stand on a grave and feel the heartbeat of a dead man! Main Street was shaping up and reminded Walter of Calico Ghost Town, where he had worked some 25 years earlier. He was determined as ever to re-create a really authentic-looking, old-time Ghost Town!

One day a man approached Walter. He looked like a page out of the Old West, wearing jeans with chaps over them, a broad-brimmed hat, and a bandana around his neck. He came to Walter and said, "I'm looking for work — I'm unemployed." Walter said, "You look like a cowboy." The fellow said, "Yes, but only in the movies. I've never really been a cowboy. But I need work, any work. I'm an honest, hard-working man, but I'm unemployed." Little did he know that he would have the chance to become one of the gunslingers and train robbers who took turns staging robberies on a train or on the stagecoach at Knott's Berry Farm.

In 1952, Walter, a train enthusiast, was offered the engines, cars and equipment from the Denver and Rio Grande Railway in Colorado, which had gone out of business. He had the steam-powered, narrow-gauge train which was built in 1881 transported to the Farm, where it was renamed the Ghost Town and Calico Railroad. It was the first time an amusement park anywhere in the world had a real operating train, and people were excited. There was a live TV broadcast by a local celebrity, Bill Welch on Channel 5, who highlighted Knott's Berry Farm for the first time over the air waves. People said, "I want to go see that train. I remember hearing about it before, and now I want to see it!" This started a real increase in the numbers of people coming to the Farm. Now, train fans came from near and far to enjoy a classic ride through the Mother Lode country, often complete with a shoot-out reenacted by trained gunslingers and train robbers.

But for many people, a favorite part of Ghost Town was the Gold Mine which Walter had built, since most Ghost Towns came about during the mid-1800s when California experienced a Gold Rush. Here, children and adults could pan for gold side by side. Then they took their precious findings to the Assay Office to have the man there appraise or determine the value of the little nuggets of "gold." He would weigh them carefully on his scale and write the amount of money they were worth on a slip of paper. Many young miners walked out of that Assay Office with a big grin on their face, feeling mighty proud of their gold claim.

Now the folks could pick up a number for their place in line to eat at Cordelia's Chicken Dinner Restaurant as they arrived at Knott's Berry Farm. They could leisurely stroll through the Ghost Town or sit on the benches scattered throughout the Farm. They noticed the prospectors pulling along their burros, whose backs were burdened by the heavy packs they carried. They would be entertained as they watched the ladies with their fancy ruffled dresses leave the Gold Trails Hotel and daintily step on the sideboard to get into the Butterfield Stagecoach, with the help of the stagecoach driver. They heard the sound of whoops coming from the saloon as some of the gamblers won their card games. The dance hall ladies could be seen through the front doors of the hotel kicking up their heels as they did the can-can dance on the stage above the bar. Visitors could even watch a melodrama at the Bird Cage Theatre, built in 1954, which was made to look just like a similar theatre in Tombstone, Arizona. Many modern-day comic actors and actresses started out in this theater, including Steve Martin.

Park visitors had to keep their ears at the ready, because when it was their turn, their number and name would be called out over the loudspeakers so they could get back to the restaurant for the chance to enjoy a fine meal with their family.

Church of Reflections

In the summer of 1955, Walter and Cordelia attended the opening ceremonies of Disneyland and were very concerned whether this new amusement park would take their business away. But when they returned to Knott's, the parking lot was totally full. They felt very grateful. Once again, they gave thanks to God for their successes. That same year, they arranged for a church that was being torn down in the neighboring town of Downey to be moved and reconstructed near Ghost Town. What was once the First Baptist Church of Downey became the "Church of Reflections." Walter and Cordelia wanted a house of worship available on site for their workers to attend before coming to work. Dean Davisson, former Knott's Publicity Director, often saw Walter and Cordelia walking to the church arm-in-arm and warmly greeting guests on Sundays. They usually settled into their favorite unmarked pew. Everyone knew it was where Mr. and Mrs. Knott were seated.

On any Sunday, a special guest currently appearing at the Goodtime Theater or someone from the Calico Saloon could replace the regular singer and musician at the Sunday service. The Sunday message was given by the in-resident minister hired by Mr. Knott, who was also available to preside over weddings highlighted by the buggy or stagecoach arrival. Mr. and Mrs. Knott took quiet personal pleasure in providing this opportunity. Since that time, many couples have exchanged their wedding vows in this quaint church, where services are still held on Sundays even today.

Soon Walter and Russell realized they also needed something for younger children to do besides strolling in Ghost Town with their parents. Walter met Bud Hurlbut around that time, and he installed the 1896 Dentzel Merry-Go-Round near the lake. He had purchased this classic ride from Hershey Park in Pennsylvania. Bud then came up with the idea to make the Calico Gold Mine Ride, which was completed in 1960. What started out as a simple two–car plan turned out to include six mine trains, with mine train tracks on three levels inside of a "mountain" that was as high as an eight-story building. The rider could see the gold miners panning in the "Glory Hole" and passed by the old dilapidated miners' shacks by the sides of the underground river, with waterfalls cascading down on either side.

Old McDonald's Animal Farm was another welcome addition which drew many families with small children. The children delighted in observing the barnyard animals and were even allowed to throw fish to feed the seals in the small pond.

In 1963, Walter had Bud build a sternwheeler boat for the Ghost Town Lake. During the ceremony to christen the boat with the name "Cordelia K.," Mrs. Knott broke a bottle of boysenberry juice against the bow. The normal custom at such events was to use champagne, but Cordelia was not in favor of anybody drinking alcohol, so she insisted on using juice. Boat builder Bud presented her with a

The "Codelia K"

dozen red roses as part of the ceremony. Eventually, a bandstand was built by the lakeside, where bands played to entertain visitors as they took a leisurely ride on the lake.

Bud Hurlbut with Mr. Knott testing the Log Ride

Later that decade, Bud proposed making a flume ride, which came to be called the Timber Mountain Log Ride and was completed in 1969. This proved to be one of the most popular rides of any at Knott's Berry Farm. Walter enjoyed the adventure of planning, building and eventually riding these and other rides. Cordelia, on the other hand, had no time or desire for going on rides. She was content to remain busy in the restaurant and kitchen.

Chapter Fourteen
Chicken and Fixings by the Numbers

A record number of chickens

In 1944, Mrs. Knott's Chicken Dinner Restaurant was able to seat 700 diners at one time. Two years later, they served their millionth chicken dinner. Just four years later, in 1950, they were serving an average of one million chicken dinners per year. One decade later, on Mother's Day in 1960, they served 8,735 dinners in one day, all made from scratch!

Only the finest milk and cream were used in the Knott's kitchen. On a typical busy Sunday, up to 200 quarts of milk were needed just to make the gravy sauce to accompany the mashed potatoes and chicken.

Walter was always supportive of what was needed for the kitchen, to make it run more efficiently so as to keep up with the demands of the crowds of customers. He invested in new-fangled machines, such as an orange juice machine that could juice a crate of oranges in less than two minutes. The machine cut the oranges, discarded the skins, separated the pulp, pumped the juice into chilled containers and then kept it fresh by agitation.

The fruit quick-freeze methods Walter had discovered and perfected allowed them to freeze 70,000 pounds of berries during the summer, which were used for making berry pies throughout the year. Walter ordered three-deck electric ovens that were roomy enough to bake 35,000 biscuits and 1,200 berry pies per day.

Mrs. Knott's kitchen also made pickles, chili sauce, French dressing, and a variety of jams and jellies and syrups from scratch. On weekends, Russell's first son Ken could be found standing on a step behind the stands of berries, ready to serve customers boysenberry punch at the tender age of eight or nine. These products were not only served fresh in the restaurant, but were also canned and offered for sale in the Berry Market and through mail order. A Holiday Assortment including three types of berry jam, plus guava and concord grape jelly in six-ounce jars could be ordered and shipped prepaid in the U.S. for as little as $1.20 at the time.

In fact, Cordelia had taught Toni's husband Kenneth Oliphant how to make jam and so the jam area became known as "Ken's Preserving Kitchen." First, he made boysenberry jam, apricot and pineapple marmalade. Second, he made pickles and salad dressings. The Knott's food line expanded to include more than 40 different types of preserves, jellies, dressings, syrups and specialty sauces and relishes.

A bustling kitchen

In the fall of 1949, a monthly newspaper was started to keep employees of Knott's Berry Farm and others informed with the latest news about their people and products. The first two volumes of "The Knotty Post" featured the details of how they prepared the chickens for serving. The chickens were delivered at night by trucks from Foster Farms, kept alive in their cages until readied for processing, then killed and transported on a chute to be scalded in hot water. A special "elevator" machine dipped them in the hot water and lifted them up automatically. Their feathers were removed by another machine, which was a large tub with rubber fingers around the edge of it. Then the chickens were singed over a gas flame, to take off the smaller pin-feathers that were still on their skins.

Under the supervision of a California State Inspector, the assembly-line process started with the chickens being hung on a moving chain and transported to "the dressing room" where about 14 ladies worked diligently to scrape the insides and put them in cold water. On a long table, the chickens were cleaned and cut up. The chicken parts were then separated into pans on a sorting table, salted, and chilled at 27 degrees. The white meat parts were submerged in very salty water, whereas the dark meat water was less salty. The pans were dated and put into the refrigerators. Later, the chicken parts were pre-cooked for 45

Processing the chickens

minutes in stainless steel pots that contained vegetable oil. Finally, they were browned in a deep frier at 375 degrees for three minutes and served.

The chicken dressing room

The poultry dressing plant at Knott's Berry Farm handled between 2500 and 3000 chickens per day during the 1950s and 1960s. Customers were able to purchase raw chickens which they could take home and cook to their liking. They were said to be very fresh. No parts of the processed chickens were wasted. The raw chicken necks and backs that were extra were sold to the California Alligator Farm across the street, to be fed to the crocodiles — about 2,000 pounds of meat each week!

In that year and many others, the Knott's Chicken Dinner Restaurant kitchen won awards for high standards of sanitation and great achievement in storing, handling, preparing and serving food in national competitions. In the first issue of "The Knotty Post," Cordelia was quoted as saying, "It has to be good because these people are our special guests and each of us in the kitchen wants, above all, to please all of these hungry people. We are proud of our kitchen and justly so."

First grandson Ken grew up to hold a very important part in the operation of the food services on the Farm, and he learned every aspect of dealing with the foods served and sold there. Beginning as a warehousing helper and truck driver, Ken was asked by Cordelia to help in the restaurant in the late 1950s. Cordelia taught him all about the food operation, both in the kitchen and also how they manufactured the Knott's products.

Like both of his grandparents, Ken had a knack for working closely with people, and was a stickler for details. He shared a special relationship with Cordelia and Walter, and became a general partner and Director of Food Administration for the Farm. Ken made decisions that affected all types of foods served throughout the Farm,

Girlsenberry with Knott's products

including the fast food stands, the Steak House, the Ghost Town Grill, the Chicken Dinner Restaurant and the bakery. As head of the Food Products Marketing Division, he worked in partnership with gourmet food stores such as the Food & Drug in Long Beach. He arranged for Knott's characters girlsenberry and boysenberry to help promote Knott's

Dennis Salts with the One-Man Band player

products. For an old fashioned days promotion, he even sent the Knott's One-Man Band. It could easily be said that grandson Ken wore a great many hats during his more than thirty years at Knott's.

Chapter Fifteen
Ever Watchful Cordelia

Keeping her eyes on the kitchen

Cordelia was always watchful of what changes could be made to please her customers. Once she noticed that some bussed plates came back to the kitchen with lots of food still on them. She thought, *I wonder why they are not eating very much meat or cabbage and ham.* On further investigation, she found out that these were plates that had been served to children. *I know what I'll do. We'll make sure the children's menu offers some vegetables that children might actually eat!* So from then on, the children's dinners at the Chicken Dinner Restaurant had less meat than the dinners served to adults, and included carrots and peas instead of cabbage and ham.

Walter and Cordelia generously served holiday dinners at Easter, Thanksgiving and Christmas to needy children. They were served jello salad, chicken, biscuits and gravy, cake and apricots. The WPA

Helping children enjoy a meal

(Work Progress Administration) usually fed them during the year. So these holiday dinners at Knott's Berry Farm were indeed a special treat for them!

WPA Children having holiday dinner

In fact, the special holiday meals became a real popular item for many folks. The turkey dinners offered at Thanksgiving, for example, included soup, turkey and dressing, mashed potatoes and giblet gravy, candied yams, vegetables, hot rolls and boysenberry jam, cranberry salad with garnish, mince meat pie, and a beverage. Many people clamored for a chance to go to Knott's Berry Farm for a special holiday dinner.

Often the kitchen was a very hectic place. It seemed like once a good routine had been set, pretty soon there were new machines to learn how to use and different routines were needed. Some of these changes were difficult for Cordelia, who enjoyed being in charge in her kitchen. The many changes were at times hard for her to accept and adjust to, but she did her best, when encouraged and supported by Walter, Ken and others. When Ken's wife Jeanette came up with the idea to start serving breakfast at the restaurant, Cordelia resisted but finally allowed a trial run. Pretty quick, Jeanette reported to Cordelia, "We're running a line." That meant there were people waiting at first five, then ten, then twenty minutes before being seated. Cordelia saw this and said, "We did the right thing!"

Cordelia gradually came to rely on others to help give her a break from the kitchen. Jeanette often picked up the slack to help out, and even served breakfast to Cordelia as she sat on the sofa in the Knott living room when Mrs. Knott was battling cancer. Betty Collier worked as Kitchen Supervisor for 46 years. These plus many others were Cordelia's eyes and ears while she stepped out of the kitchen. They carried on her watchful traditions in order to make sure that everything ran smoothly and without glitches.

Though the kitchen work was very time-consuming, Cordelia always took the time to cook dinner for Walter. At times, when grandson Stephen helped in the Berry Market, the customers detected the aroma of Cordelia's cooking coming from their house right behind the market. Sometimes it smelled like string beans with bacon, at other times, like rice meat loaf or some other delicious dish. The people Stephen was helping asked if what they smelled could be purchased. They were often surprised and shocked to hear that Cordelia was cooking up something for her and Mr. Knott for dinner. Walter knew who was calling him if his phone rang at 5 p.m. Cordelia insisted that he be home and ready to eat at that time, or else she would call him. If he was in the middle of talking with someone, he often said, "Excuse me, I must go. Madam is waiting supper on me." And every night after dinner, Walter helped out by drying the dishes.

Cordelia also took time to make ice box cookies for her children and grandchildren's families. Russell's wife Millie was glad to receive these cookie loaves which were very tasty and could be refrigerated. She was amazed that Cordelia had time to make cookies between all her kitchen duties.

Chapter Sixteen
A Gal Named "Pam"

Linda "Pam" Elliott

More and more young people in the Buena Park and Orange County area were being employed by Knott's Berry Farm and at the Chicken Dinner Restaurant as it continued to expand and grow. Often they were high school or college students. In the restaurant, Cordelia had them work as partners so that they could cover for each other when they were due for a break, especially on busy Sundays.

One day in 1956, a 32 year-old recently divorced mother named Linda Elliott came to the Knott's Employment Office looking for a job. The people working there said, "We don't hire anyone over 30." Surprised, Linda was distressed, as she had two young daughters and herself to support. She knew that she could not give up, as she had tried to land a job at several other places already. Undaunted, Linda went to the Chicken Dinner Restaurant and shared her predicament with Cordelia, who hired her on the spot. *She looks like a very fit young lady, and has such a nice, friendly smile,* Cordelia thought.

On being hired as a waitress, Cordelia said to Linda, "We already have someone working here as a server by the name of Linda, so we'll call you 'Pam'." And that was her name from then on at work. It was important that all of the waitresses had different names, since the meal orders came down the line with one of their names on it, to signify which table it should head to. Pam, as she would become known by her fellow workers and by her customers, was assigned to serve in the section of the restaurant just to the east of the kitchen, and that was her station for the more than 50 years that she ended up working at the Chicken Dinner Restaurant!

When she began, Pam had to buy a cotton dress with short sleeves to wear to work. Later on, she was given a green dress with a white collar that had puff sleeves with white cuffs that came to the elbow, and a French maid apron. Her hair was pulled back with a matching-colored bow holding it up. Comfortable white polished shoes completed the outfit, and were essential, since she would be on her feet many hours a day.

Pam soon noticed that everyone specialized in the kitchen. If you did biscuits, you just did that. The biscuits were made by hand. The biscuit-makers, such as Edith Valentine, cut out the biscuits using Cordelia's original cutter, put them into oil, then dipped them in flour. The pie-makers made the dough for the pies in a big washtub. The dough was then put through a wringer to flatten it.

Cordelia was an excellent cook who loved the kitchen. She never needed to look at a recipe; she just knew what combinations would taste good, such as string beans with bacon, which she often cooked at home for Walter. She used a pastry wheel to cut off the excess pastry and decorate

Cordelia trimming pie crust

the edges of her famous boysenberry pies. She often modeled for her workers what she expected them to do. One of her faithful pie-makers was Lois Story, who worked in the kitchen for almost 30 years, and whose daughter Barbara Wharton ended up working for son Russell and Knott's Berry Farm for more than 30 years.

As Pam hurriedly came through the kitchen to pick up the meals she was serving, she often saw Cordelia sitting next to her trusted helper Margie Hall. The waitresses would give their orders to Cordelia and then Margie wrote them up; including

Dish washers

the special request orders. Some people wanted all white or all dark meat, for example. Mrs. Knott and Margie watched closely over the trays going out of the kitchen into the dining rooms. If they saw that a plate with mashed potatoes and milk gravy looked messy, they'd have that tray removed from the line-up and the potatoes were replaced.

When she began working at the restaurant, the other waitresses warned Pam that Mrs. Knott would not stand for any monkey business. It seemed to them like Cordelia could see things that none of the rest of them could, because if someone did something wrong, she'd point it out right away and expect them to fix it. She had the keenest eyes and wouldn't put up with wastefulness. If the waitresses dipped their glasses into the ice bin to get ice, instead of using a metal scoop, Cordelia got very angry. That was unsanitary and there was the danger of the glasses breaking. Besides, those glasses cost money! Plus the ice bin had to be checked for broken glass, and that took valuable time away from the customers being served.

Cordelia was a stickler about other things as well. When the hustle and bustle of the kitchen became especially hectic, she was even seen going out into the alley to look for spilled silverware, when she thought the servers might have accidentally dropped some into the trash bins as they were clearing tables. She watched her servers closely, and if one of them was dishonest, they could get fired on the spot!

Though Pam noticed how strict Cordelia was with her workers, she worked hard to please "Mama Knott" and came to love her. Pam came to know how generous and kind Mrs. Knott was when she saw a need. Pam's fellow waitress Aileen Leithead was also a single parent, and sometimes, at the end of her shift, Cordelia would quietly call her over and say "Here, Aileen, take this extra chicken home to your mom and son." Many other workers had similar experiences over the years.

Jackie Jackson, who had been hired ten years before Pam, was one of several waitresses who were privileged to spend the night upstairs with the Knott family if the weather outside was too foggy for safe driving. Cordelia had extra nightgowns on hand and ready for just such occasions. Irene Dunn noticed that Cordelia was especially concerned about a fellow waitress's trouble, as her young daughter had been badly burned in a home fire. Mrs. Knott repeatedly asked about the girl's progress through the extensive surgeries she had to withstand. Betty Valentine, known as Val, shared that her brother needed to see a specialist because he needed elbow surgery. One day, Cordelia quietly called Val's mother Edith away from her task of making biscuits and put several hundred dollars into the palm of her hand. She made it clear that she did not want to be repaid.

It was these special heart-warming gestures that endeared Cordelia to those around her. It was no wonder, then, that many of the Chicken Dinner Restaurant workers stayed on for a number of years, often anywhere from ten to forty or more years! Indeed, many workers enjoyed their jobs and spoke so highly of the Knott family that other family members came to work at Knott's Berry Farm as well. Chicken helper Helen Rogers, for example, named one of her daughters after Cordelia. Her children Ralph, Carol, Shirley and Sandra all worked in the kitchen at one time or another.

Pam felt Cordelia was like a typical grandma. At times, when an employee complimented her on her earrings or another piece of jewelry she wore, at the end of the day it was theirs to keep. One evening, fellow waitress Marie "Rita" Gauldin was the last employee to finish her shift. Left alone with Mrs. Knott in the kitchen, she felt led to say to her, "You know, I don't know a thing about you." Cordelia invited her into the Knott house and it was like a step back in time. There was a huge dark mahogany table, old-fashioned light fixtures, and many other antiques. Even though her children had tried to convince her many times to buy more modern furniture, Cordelia explained, "This is my home and I like it the way it is." She would much rather spend money on her business and on her workers than on getting new things for her house and herself. At the end of the night, Cordelia gave Rita a wallet-sized wedding picture, which she cherished and showed off many times to others.

Being a person who likes people, Pam enjoyed going to the Christmas parties that were held at Laura Jenk's home. She got

Cordelia enjoyed get-togethers with her workers

to know Cordelia on a more personal level when she was able to chat with her off duty on such occasions. In fact, when Cordelia came down with breast cancer in her last years, she asked Pam to help her out by sewing special wide sleeves onto her blouses and dresses so that she could move her arms more easily. Rarely did Cordelia humble herself to ask for help, so Pam felt honored to be a real friend to her by helping out in this personal matter.

Chapter Seventeen
The Golden Rule Works Wonders

Walter enjoys rewarding workers

Pam was one of many workers who were loyal to the Knott family because of how well they were treated as employees. Both Walter and Cordelia insisted on following the Golden Rule themselves and they expected the same of their workers. In his monthly "Knotty Post" columns, Walter reminded employees to treat others as they themselves would want to be treated. Because of their steady efforts to succeed in the desert and since then, Walter and Cordelia had a strong belief in the value of hard work. They held high expectations for their children and those whom they employed, because they knew that honest efforts reap great rewards. But they always treated others fairly and with respect. Walter felt that good will was more valuable than anything sold at Knott's Berry Farm.

Cordelia and Walter both took a personal interest in their workers and often were open to listening to new ideas. Walter's office door was always open and he was ready to listen to other people's thoughts. If you had good ideas and were willing to work at them, they would encourage you to try. They would give you the things you needed to try out your ideas, and then later, they gave you all the credit for your new ideas.

Back when the Chicken Dinner Restaurant had started serving breakfasts, Cordelia had asked Pam, "Do you want to serve breakfast and lunch, or lunch and dinner?" Pam replied that she would prefer lunch and dinner, since she knew from experience that some of the early morning diners who were truckers or travelers were often grouchy and hard to deal with because they had been on the road for many hours. She was grateful that Cordelia had given her a choice. Pam realized that Mrs. Knott was a firm believer in higher education and often gave her workers some leeway when it came to work hours. She would tailor working hours in the restaurant to fit the class schedules of the college-age young people who worked for her.

Workers were well rewarded for their hard work and good ideas. By October 1950, a total of about $41,000 dollars had been given to 600 employees in bonuses. This was money given to workers according to how much profit or extra money had been made during the previous year. Mr. Knott also set up a profit-sharing-retirement plan whereby workers could be like partners in the business, and reap monetary rewards that were put into a special fund to be paid to them when they left Knott's, or when they were older and needed the money to live on. It gave the Knott family great joy to share the success of the Farm with those who worked for them. As Walter stated in the "Knotty Post", "I am awfully anxious to surprise you with a larger share of profits this fall. Give me all the help you can, but above all be good to our customers."

Both Walter and Cordelia were very generous to their employees. For every five years of employment, the workers were given recognition at an awards party, and for those who had worked a long time, watches, special rings, and lapel pins were given. Pam ended up receiving a ring with rubies and a covered wagon after working at the Chicken Dinner Restaurant for 35 years, a special $1,000 bonus at forty years, and a special recognition when she had worked there for half a century! Cordelia especially enjoyed these awards parties and the potlucks given for current and former employees. In July of 1959, for example, Cordelia was happy to see 100 current and former employees take part. One of those people was Hazel Harvey, who was her original biscuit-maker that had worked in the kitchen in 1934.

Employee thanks Mrs. Knott for award

Besides the awards, bonuses and profit sharing, the Knott family gave workers a gift of food at the holidays. At Christmas time in 1959, employees got to choose whether they wanted a free ham, turkey, or a dozen assorted jams and jellies. This became an annual custom and a well-loved tradition at Knott's Berry Farm.

In 1961, Walter and Cordelia celebrated their 50th year of marriage. Across Beach Boulevard from Knott's Berry Farm

The Golden Raintree Plaque

near Independence Hall, a replica of which Walter built, stands a cluster of tall trees. Beneath them rests a plaque which states, "The Golden Rain Trees presented to Walter and Cordelia Knott on their Golden Wedding Anniversary, June 3, 1961, from Knott's Employees and Concessionaires." This gift stands as a testament to the feelings of mutual respect which the Knott family and their employees held for each other.

Chapter Eighteen
Patriots and Politics

Nixon at the Berry Farm

Walter and Cordelia believed in our country and were strong patriots. Back in the early 1940s, Walter had encouraged young boys and girls across the nation to plant victory gardens. He understood that a nation which can produce its own food will not grow hungry or need to depend on other countries. In an article for young readers entitled "Wanted: Food", Walter ended with these words: "Help hurry Victory. Remember, Food means Freedom." He also had planted a victory demonstration garden as an example for others to follow. The Knott's Nursery gave out brochures which told what, when, and how to plant, including pictures and drawings. In this way, Walter hoped to encourage young people to have an independent spirit, just like other innovative farmers such as George Washington and Luther Burbank.

Ghost Town Rotary Club

As a citizen, Walter was active in the Buena Park community. He was an Honorary Member of the Buena Park Rotary Club, which met at the Chicken Dinner Restaurant starting in 1955. He was given this honor by the Rotary Club because he conducted himself in his business by the ideas of their oath, called the 4-Way Test: "Is it the truth? Is it fair to all concerned? Will it build goodwill and better friendships? Will it be beneficial to all concerned?" Since the Rotary Club had members from many different businesses, Walter became friends with people from all walks of life. This was one of many organizations in which he became active.

Although he was naturally shy and didn't enjoy speaking to large crowds, Walter joined Toastmasters and was determined to have some of his views heard. He was passionate about wanting to preserve the ideals upon which this country was founded, and was troubled when he saw that people were acting like they didn't care what direction our country was taking.

Walter was beginning to get involved in politics because of his strong belief in our freedoms and our American system. In the early 1960s, Walter was appointed to the Republican Central Committee. He looked up to Abraham Lincoln, who was one of the first candidates for president sponsored by the Republican Party, just about 100 years earlier. Walter didn't wish to run for political office, but wanted to support candidates who he could tell were solid, reliable citizens and who held the same beliefs in limited government and free enterprise as did both he and Cordelia.

Walter was appointed as a representative to attend the Republican National Convention held in Chicago in 1960. When Walter asked Cordelia about traveling along with him, she thought to herself, *Why would I want to go all the way to Chicago, and listen to a lot of speakers? Besides, will the restaurant be okay while I'm away? I don't want to come back to a mess!* But finally she reluctantly agreed.

Once there, Cordelia enjoyed herself and was sad to see the time go by so fast. On more than one occasion, she met with other ladies and shared with them about how she had started a tea room that eventually became a restaurant. When they were amazed at her story about how many regular customers they had, she said to them, "Yes, we do have a farm, and we do serve dinners." Cordelia invited the ladies to come to the Farm for a visit, and many of them did just that.

Also in that same year, Walter and Cordelia arranged a big event at Knott's Berry Farm for Richard Nixon, who was running for president. "Picnic with Dick" was a big success, where 25,000 people were served about 10,000 box lunches, all organized by the Chicken Dinner Restaurant under the guidance of Cordelia.

In 1961, Walter was honored by the Orange County Board of Supervisors for forty years of service to the community, county, and the country. They designated a certain day as "Walter Knott Day" in honor of him. Cordelia was very proud of him! Walter said, "Cordy, they wouldn't be honoring me if it weren't for your support. You're my partner in all of this."

It was after the 1960 Republican Convention in Chicago that Walter had started to dream about building Independence Hall.

Independence Hall

In 1963, he took a trip to Philadelphia to view the building where the founding fathers had originally drafted our Declaration of Independence, and he was moved by that experience. After many years of plans, building permits and approvals, and further visits back east to Philadelphia, the dedication of the brick-by-brick replica of Independence Hall took place on July 4, 1966. This was a dream come true for Walter.

The Liberty Bell

The main centerpiece inside Knott's Independence Hall is a 2,000 pound Liberty Bell, which Bud (designer of the log ride) offered to make for the Knott family. After a visit to Philadelphia to measure the real bell, Bud got to work reproducing it. The biggest challenge turned out to be trying to get the crack in the bell to be just like the crack in the original.

On Dedication Day, Walter expressed pride in his American heritage and stated that Independence Hall and the Liberty Bell are America's greatest symbols of freedom. He was excited that many people and school children would now be able to come and touch the Liberty Bell and see where our great documents were signed, without having to travel all the way to Philadelphia.

Chapter Nineteen
The Biggest Event

A time to celebrate!

Another decade had gone by since their celebration of being married for 50 years, and here it was, ten years later, June of 1971, when Walter and Cordelia were able to look back on 60 years of being married! A dear friend of theirs, Ronald Reagan, celebrated with them. He was then serving his second term as Governor of California.

The biggest event ever held on the Farm, as described in "The Knotty Post" employee newsletter, was when the 2,100-seat John Wayne Theatre was opened on June 19, 1971. Marion Knott and her husband Dwight "Andy" Anderson had the idea to make a

Gypsy Camp and had brought it up at one of the Knott family sessions. Walter and Cordelia made it a habit to hold family gatherings every Thursday morning in their parlor to set policy, solve problems, and plan for the future. After the family considered and approved the idea of a Gypsy Camp, it was decided to also include plans for a new theatre. This was a building project that was completed within a mere nine months. Marion's son Darryl became the Director of Entertainment for the theatre and arranged many fine performances by well-known entertainment artists.

At the grand opening event, California Governor Ronald Reagan introduced Mr. and Mrs. Knott and presided over the ceremonies, along with actor John Wayne. Many words of praise and recognition were spoken about Walter and Cordelia Knott. Walter, in turn, expressed sincere appreciation and admiration for John Wayne as someone who was not afraid to stand up and defend his beliefs. During the ceremony, John Wayne presented Cordelia with an armful of pink roses and recognized her as the "Queen of the Kitchen!" In his foreword to the biography of Walter Knott called *Keeper of the Flame*, John Wayne wrote: "The lives of Walter Knott and his wonderful wife paint a picture of America at its best. We are proud of them."

Since that time, this theatre had been renamed the Good Time Theatre, and is currently called the Charles M. Schulz Theatre, recognizing the creator of Snoopy. Many country western and popular performers have been highlighted at this theatre since it was built.

John Wayne and Ronald Reagan were not the only famous people who came to Knott's Berry Farm. Many entertainers and other VIP's were performers and/or visitors over the years, including Jerry Lewis, Jonathan Winters, Elizabeth Taylor and Eddy Fisher, Eve Arden, George Murphy, Dorothy Dandridge, Rudy

Service with a smile!

Vallee, Connie Stevens, Lucille Ball, Donnie and Marie Osmond, Harriet and Ricky Nelson, Burt Reynolds, Jane Russell, Natalie Wood, Charles Bronson, Amos and Andy, and Chuck Norris. Many of these patrons enjoyed coming for a meal at Cordelia's Chicken Dinner Restaurant. Pam Elliott noted that she was able to shake hands with John Wayne, and that comedian Jonathan Winters was very forgiving when she accidentally spilled milk on him while being his waitress. Rita Gauldin shared that Lucille Ball loved Mrs. Knott's chicken. Her limousine would stop in front of the restaurant by special arrangement to pick up chicken-to-go. Rita also shared that the South African diamond merchant DeBeers was someone she served, as well as an Indian princess who was heavily protected by body guards.

Chapter Twenty
A Life Well-Lived

Paul Von Klieben painting of Mrs. Knott with her kitchen

The year was now 1973. The Chicken Dinner Restaurant had eight dining rooms and could serve 1,130 diners at one time. The charge for the full traditional chicken dinner meal was just $3.50. When interviewed by a *Los Angeles Times* news reporter in December of that year, Cordelia proudly stated, "I don't know anywhere you can get as good a meal for the money." She had stepped out of active management of the Chicken Dinner Restaurant for the first time that year, but still kept a close check on the operation. Marion Knott said that Cordelia was shy but very strict when it came to business. "My mother was in the kitchen all the time. She taught them the values of doing what they were supposed to do." By this time, Marion and her sister Toni had added their own touch to the Farm by opening Marion and Toni's Sport Shop, where fine women's clothing was sold.

Ken, Russell's son and the oldest grandson of Walter and Cordelia, described how Cordelia was at age 82. She was still active in the restaurant two times daily, using a black cane to steady herself as she walked among the big stainless steel vats holding the frying oil for the chicken. In the evenings, she sat at the kitchen desk. At that time, Ken controlled the Chicken Dinner Restaurant and all other food services at the Farm. Mrs. Knott told the *Times* reporter that she was not worried about the future of her restaurant. She was very confident about her grandson Ken running it, and expressed pride in him and the other children and grandchildren. "Everything will be all right in their hands," she said.

During the *Times* interview, Cordelia reminisced about how she had started the restaurant: "We had some bills to pay and didn't know where the money was coming from... I got this idea of selling fried chicken dinners in the Tea Room. I surprised Dad when I told him about it one day... He didn't object, but I think he had some doubts. I charged 65 cents for the dinner and we served eight that day. Business grew like topsy and I never dreamed what would happen."

Stephen Knott, youngest son of Russell, after his first job of opening the Chapel door, had a variety of jobs on the Farm. He worked at one time or another as a street sweeper, chicken truck helper (for which he had to get up at 3 a.m.), on the grounds crew to clean up the grounds, in the Preserving Department making jams and jellies, as a clerk and merchandising helper in the Berry Market, as a host in the Steak House, and as head of the Security Department.

Stephen described his grandmother Cordelia as a great mother. "She was a true pioneer who proved herself to be that, when she lived alone in Newbury," he said, "when they built their own house there, and were so far away from the neighbors that they had to be truly self-sufficient." Stephen described how he enjoyed sitting with his grandmother and grandfather on the benches by the side of the Chicken Dinner Restaurant in the late afternoons, watching the visitors and talking with them. Cordelia loved to visit the Candy Store, but had to be more careful now, since she was diabetic. Of all the sweet jams and jellies produced at the Farm, Cordelia loved grape jelly the best.

On April 23, 1974, Cordelia Hornaday Knott passed away in Buena Park at the age of 84, after she lost her battle with cancer. Under her guidance, the Chicken Dinner Restaurant named after her had already been successful for forty years. Many of her waitresses and other Knott's employees spoke highly of Cordelia. It would take many pages to recount their praises.

Walter Knott died seven years after Cordelia, on December 3, 1981. He was just one week shy of turning 92, and had endured Parkinson's disease for more than twenty years. Flags were lowered to half-staff at the news of his death. Both Cordelia and Walter were buried at Loma Vista Memorial Park in Fullerton.

Cordelia was more cautious than Walter when approaching new ideas, but she shared with him the belief that dreams can be made real by hard work and earnest efforts. Walter's saying that both of them lived by was:

"Whatever we vividly imagine,

ardently desire, sincerely believe,

and enthusiastically act upon…

must inevitably come to pass!"

Afterword

Cordelia & Walter Knott's Legacy Continues

50th Anniversary line for Mrs. Knott's Chicken Dinner – 1984

At the Knott's 50th Year Anniversary Celebration of the Chicken Dinner Restaurant, the Knott family allowed people to pay the original price of $.65 for the full meal, just like when Mrs. Knott's first served chicken dinners on her wedding china in 1934. People lined up six-people-wide, some waiting up to six hours, to taste Cordelia's famous chicken dinner. The line wrapped around the perimeter of Knott's Berry Farm.

Where Fried Chicken is King

Marion Knott with 1940s Pie Tin

When interviewed by the "Orange County Register" during the 75th Anniversary Year of the Chicken Dinner Restaurant, Marion Knott stated, "I'm very grateful that my family was able to create something that has lasted… A lot of it was plain old luck. Dad told you he was only a farmer. But he had vision, and that's what it took." Marion is the only surviving child of Walter and Cordelia.

The Chicken Dinner Restaurant continues to be a historical

landmark where fried chicken is king. This one-of-a-kind place is now capable of serving more than 1200 diners at a time. The restaurant dishes up 1.5 million meals per year to their hungry, faithful customers.

The Cordelia Knott Center for Wellness in Orange, California

In October 2002, a non-profit facility was established in nearby Orange, California, to support medical care for cancer patients. It was given the name The Cordelia Knott Center for Wellness in honor of Mrs. Knott. When dedicating the facility, oldest daughter

Cordelia Knott in 1967

Virginia Knott had this to say about her mother: "Throughout her life, my mother, Cordelia Hornaday Knott, showed other women how to give. Her humble spirit, her generosity, and her hard work are legendary. It is with much love and gratitude that this Center for Wellness is dedicated to her memory. My mother would have been deeply honored by this recognition." Virginia Bender Knott passed away in 2003.

Cordelia Knott

Walter's Legacy

Walter Knott lived on for seven years past the death of his beloved wife Cordelia. He passed away one week before his 92nd birthday, on December 3, 1981. He had endured Parkinson's disease for more than twenty years. He was known as "Mr. Republican" in the Orange County area. Flags throughout Orange County were lowered to half-staff at the news of his death.

Independence Hall

Still open and free to tourists and school groups alike, Independence Hall makes Knott's Berry Farm unique. "Walter Knott came from pioneer stock...[He] believed that those frontier, pioneer experiences made America what it is. He wanted to...make sure people remembered their history, and it worked. People came from all over just to visit ghost town and have themselves a chicken dinner. The berry farm had become a theme park. For Walter Knott, our history as a democracy was part of what makes America great, just like the Old West."

Independence Hall

– Phil Brigandi, O.C. Historian and Archivist

Walter Knott at Calico

Calico Ghost Town

Calico was a real boom town that produced silver and borax from 1881 until 1907. Then it lay dormant until 1951, when Walter purchased it and refurbished the general store, bottle house, old school house, Boot

87

Hill Cemetery, print shop, pottery works and the Maggie Mine. He donated the site to San Bernardino County in 1966, and Calico is now a regional park with a professional historian on staff in the Visitor's Center. Other features include the crooked house, a large cauldron labeled as a Chinese bathtub, a cable tram, and staged gunfights.

Posing in the Picture Gallery

Quotes

"I never saw my mother look in a cookbook. She just knew what to do, how to combine things to make them taste good."

   – Marion Knott, youngest of four Knott children

"Knott's Berry Farm was a fun place to work for both of my sons. Mama Knott was a wonderful mother-in-law to me, and she loved her family very much."

   – Millie Knott, Russell Knott's wife

"My grandmother Cordelia was a super person and a lady. She was meticulous, observant, determined, and had lots of stamina. She taught me every aspect of the restaurant and food business."

   – Ken Knott, son of Russell Knott

"Cordelia was an excellent cook and loved being in the kitchen. She made up her own recipes for making jams and jellies. She cared about her workers very much. She even went to jail to bail out waitresses."

   – Stephen Knott, Ken's younger brother

"Mrs. Knott was a businesswoman to the core."

   – Jeanette Knott, wife of oldest grandson Ken

"After people complimented Cordelia on her jewelry, she would give it to them. Finally, they decided to compliment her on what she wore, rather than on jewelry which she could more easily remove and give away."

   – Patsy Marshall, former Knott's employee and Buena Park City Council member

"Some of us called her 'Mama Knott' because she was a wonderful, typical grandma. She was kind and fair, and loved watching the people who came to visit the farm."

  – Linda "Pam" Elliott, waitress in the Chicken Dinner Restaurant for 51 years

"The Knott family was wonderful to work for. Those were the best years of my life."

  – Barbara Wharton, former employee of Knott's

"Mr. Knott made his own breakfast of oatmeal. On one of his daily walks in Ghost Town, he stopped by the Grist Mill. He asked the miller for some wheat grain to be ground just fine enough to be ready to make his cereal. In the evening, he would take a small sauce pan, add water and let it set overnight. It was ready to cook the next morning."

  – Dean Davisson, former Knott's Publicity Director

"Walter was aware of the need for change. He was the consummate change advocate and pragmatist. He recognized that if you don't change, you lose ground."

  – Kirk Real, Berry Market merchandising expert and Knott's employee for more than 53 years

"The Knott family's generosity was again demonstrated when they sold the Farm to Cedar Fair. Those of us who worked there full time and part time over the years received a very nice monetary gift along with a warm note of thanks. The size of the gift was based on hours worked and years of service, so many people received in the thousands of dollars!"

  – Irv Trinkle, former Berry Market employee

"Cordelia and Walter went to Hawaii for 3-week vacations some summers, but Cordelia always wanted to cut it short and come back early. She missed her friends in the kitchen. The kitchen was her life. The camaraderie in the kitchen was a reflection of the Knott family. I don't think I would have loved working anywhere as much."

- Marie "Rita" Gauldin, waitress in the Chicken Dinner Restaurant for 38 years

"I first went to Knott's in 1941. We used to enjoy going on the merry-go-round when it was on the other side of Beach Blvd. We'd have a picnic and feed the ducks on the pond."

- Donna Bagley, prominent Buena Park historian

"I was so touched when I used to see Cordelia and Walter walking hand–in–hand under the wisteria vine that hung on the trellis by Virginia's Gift Shop. They were headed home after their evening stroll through the Farm."

- Laurie Olson, longtime Buena Park resident

Photos

Baby Virginia

Berry Stand

Knott Children – 1930

Walter Knott at his desk

Knott's Berry Farm stand

Walter and Cordelia at the Gold Trails Hotel

Knott's Berry Place – 1933

Cashier – 1940

Knott Family in the Rock Garden – 1940

Cook frying the chicken – 1940s

Mother's Day – 1944

Walter and Waitresses – 1940

93

Making pies – 1949

Chicken Dinner Restaurant

Sailors enjoy meal – 1950

Chicken Dinner Restaurant – 1950

Chicken Dinner Waitresses

Knott Family Photo

Walter & Cordelia viewing the remodel – 1951

Calico Mine Ride – 1960

Chicken Dinner Restaurant interior – 1960

Waitress Halloween – 1960

Cordelia Knott

Prospector's Day Parade – 1972

Knott Family – 1970

Walter & Cordelia – 1970

Walter & Cordelia posing for a postcard

Chicken Dinner Restaurant interior – 1989

Walter, Cordelia & Grandchildren on float

Linda "Pam" Elliott

"Pam" Celebrating her retirement with Snoopy

Carol serving Chicken

Chicken Dinner – 1990

Mrs. Knott's Restaurant & Bakery

Chicken Processor

Current Photos

The author and her husband with Marion Knott

Christiane Salts and Stephen Knott

Marty Keithley, Dennis Salts, and John Wray

Georgette and Dean Davisson, Patsy Marshall, Carolyn Carey, and Marta Armstrong

Kirk Real in the Berry Market

Don Prescott with military families

Acknowledgements

Knott's Berry Farm has grown and grown over the years. It currently covers more than 185 acres. Even though the Knott family no longer owns the Farm, new owner Cedar Fair, L.P., continues to carry on the Knott spirit of hard work and down-home hospitality. Countless anonymous gifts and resources have been given to the community in the name of the Knott family.

I would like to acknowledge the following people who are currently working at Knott's Berry Farm and freely gave me assistance and advice: Marty Keithley, Knott's General Manager and gunslinger of yore, for the referrals and contacts; Don Prescott, Knott's Resort Hotel Manager, for his assistance; John Wray, Manager of the Chicken Dinner Restaurant, for his tours of the kitchen and contacts with "Pam" and other key people; Jennifer Blazey, Publicity Director, for direction and publishing advice; Kirk Real, for his interesting stories; and Allen Palovik, Reprographics Supervisor, for assistance with photos. Former employees of Knott's who lent a hand were Patsy Marshall and Dean Davisson, who both have served Knott's in the Publicity Department; Irv Trinkle, who worked in the Merchandising Division; and of course Linda "Pam" Elliott and all the other wonderful waitresses, waiters, bus boys, and servers who have opened up to me in sharing the memories of their work life in the Chicken Dinner Restaurant.

Marion Knott and Cordelia and Walter's grandsons Ken and Stephen Knott have been most gracious in sharing with me and answering my numerous questions about Cordelia and the Farm. I am grateful for the time they spent with me on the phone and in person to give their blessing for this project.

I am indebted to Phil Brigandi and Chris Jepsen at the Orange County Archives, for allowing me to access and peruse the collections stored there which the Knott family, Cedar Fair and Jack Falfas kindly donated. Michael Mello of the O.C. Register has covered Knott's news in several informative articles over the past few years. I thank the Buena Park Library for providing access to their historical collection of Knott's memorabilia, including the Ghost Town News and Knotty Post publications covering 1941 to 1975. Thank you to Louise Mazerov, Bruce Pasarow, and Mary Ivelia, who provided access, advice and editorial assistance.

Most of all, I wish to thank my Lord for providing me with the idea of doing this project, and for giving me the initiative, determination and stamina to see it to completion. My team of prayer partners gave me their support and prayers. I thank my sister Uta and mother Victoria for their loving encouragement. My husband Dennis helped immeasurably with his advice, patience, and technical assistance. My daughters Carrie and Tracy also gave me their valuable input. And thank you, Richard, for your invaluable assistance with the cover and design of this book.

Christiane Victoria Salts

Bibliography

Print

Caldwell, Willie Mae. The Genealogy of the Knott Family, 1617–1989: Founders of Knott's Berry Farm. La Habra, California: 1989.

Chamberlin, H.A. "From Coyotes to Commerce" B.P. News Independent [Buena Park]. 2/72–4/73. Print.

Harris, Richard. Early Amusement Parks of Orange County. San Francisco, California: Arcadia Publishing, 2008.

Holmes, Roger and Paul Bailey. Fabulous Farmer – The Story of Walter Knott and His Berry Farm. Los Angeles, California: Westernlore Publishers, 1956.

Knott's Historical Holdings. "Ghost Town News", "Knotty News", "The Knotty Post", "The Berry Vine". Published at Knott's Berry Farm: Buena Park Library, 1941 – Present.

Knott's Historical Holdings. MS. Orange County Historical Archives.

Kooiman, Helen. "Walter Knott: Keeper of the Flame" Fullerton, California: Plycon Press, 1973.

Los Angeles Times. Print.

Nygaard, Norman. Walter Knott, Twentieth Century Pioneer. Grand Rapids, Michigan: Zondervan Publishing, 1965.

Sikking, Florine and Judith Zeidler. Knott's Berry Farm Cookbook. Los Angeles, California: Armstrong Publishing, 1976.

Web sites

Buena Park Historical Society. Web. 02 Aug. 2009. <http://www.historicalsociety.org>.

Calico Ghost Town, an Old West Mining Adventure in California. Web. 02 Aug. 2009. <http://www.calicotown.com/index.php>.

Knott's Berry Farm – America's 1st Theme Park! Web. 02 Aug. 2009. <http://www.knotts.com>.

Orange County Historical Archives. Clerk–Recorder – Tom Daly. Web. 02 Aug. 2009. <http://www.ocrecorder.com/Archives/arhistry.asp>.

Orange County Register Newspaper Archive. Web. 02 Aug. 2009. <http://www.ocregister.com>.

The Knott's Berry Farm Museum. Jay Jennings. Web. 02 Aug. 2009. <http://www.knottsberryfarm.blogspot.com/>.

Photos

Edey, Maitland A. This Fabulous Century, Vol. 1: 1900–1910. New York, NY Time Life Books 1969. Pages 12 and 14.

Jennings, Jay <http://www.knottsberryfarm.blogspot.com/>. Page 42.

LeRoy Bi-Centennial Commission. Heritage of the Prairie. Kramer Publishing Company, 1976. Page 7.